Explore Ancient Rome

Zelda Wagner

Lerner Publications ◆ Minneapolis

Lerner Publications Company
An imprint of Lerner Publishing Group, Inc.
241 First Avenue North
Minneapolis, MN 55401 USA

For reading levels and more information, look up this title at www.lernerbooks.com.

Main body text set in Billy Infant Regular. Typeface provided by SparkyType.

Editor: Evan Villas **Photo Editor:** Lucien Brinkley
Lerner team: Angel Kidd

Library of Congress Cataloging-in-Publication Data

Names: Wagner, Zelda, 2000- author
Title: Explore Ancient Rome / Zelda Wagner.
Description: Minneapolis, MN : Lerner Publications, 2026. | Series: Lightning bolt books— Early civilizations | Includes bibliographical references and index. | Audience: Ages 6-9 | Audience: Grades 2-3 | Summary: "Ancient Rome was one of the most powerful civilizations of all time. It was home to tens of millions of people! Readers will discover the daily lives and cultures of some of these people"— Provided by publisher.
Identifiers: LCCN 2025018315 (print) | LCCN 2025018316 (ebook) | ISBN 9798765689288 library binding | ISBN 9798348028978 paperback | ISBN 9798765696828 epub
Subjects: LCSH: Rome—Civilization—Juvenile literature
Classification: LCC DG77 .W346 2025 (print) | LCC DG77 (ebook) | DDC 937—dc23/eng/20250708

LC record available at https://lccn.loc.gov/2025018315
LC ebook record available at https://lccn.loc.gov/2025018316

Manufactured in the United States of America
1-1012505-54796-8/9/2025

Table of Contents

Rise of Rome

A small village formed about three thousand years ago. At first, Rome was like any other village. But it soon became the center of one of the world's greatest civilizations.

Ancient Rome was near the Tiber River in central Italy. Travelers and traders often stopped there. Rome grew into a busy city.

Only men served in the ancient Roman army.

The Romans believed their gods wanted them to rule over the whole world. They used their army to take over most of what we now call Italy.

About two thousand years ago, Rome became an empire.

An empire is a large area where people are ruled by one person.

A statue of Emperor Augustus in Rome

Augustus was Rome's first emperor. Under his rule, Rome became the most powerful civilization in the world. It spread to Europe, Africa, and Asia.

Ancient Romans

Everyone in the Roman Empire had a role. The people who owned land were the richest. Some became senators who made laws.

Most Romans worked as farmers, builders, and craftspeople. Some became soldiers who fought with spears, swords, and shields to expand the empire.

Workers build a wall in ancient Rome.

A Roman farmer with an ox

Farmers grew wheat and other grains. They also grew fruits and vegetables, including carrots, peas, grapes, and apricots. They used oxen to prepare their fields.

The Romans enjoyed sports such as gladiator fights and chariot racing. They wore gold and bronze jewelry. They prayed at temples lined with huge stone columns.

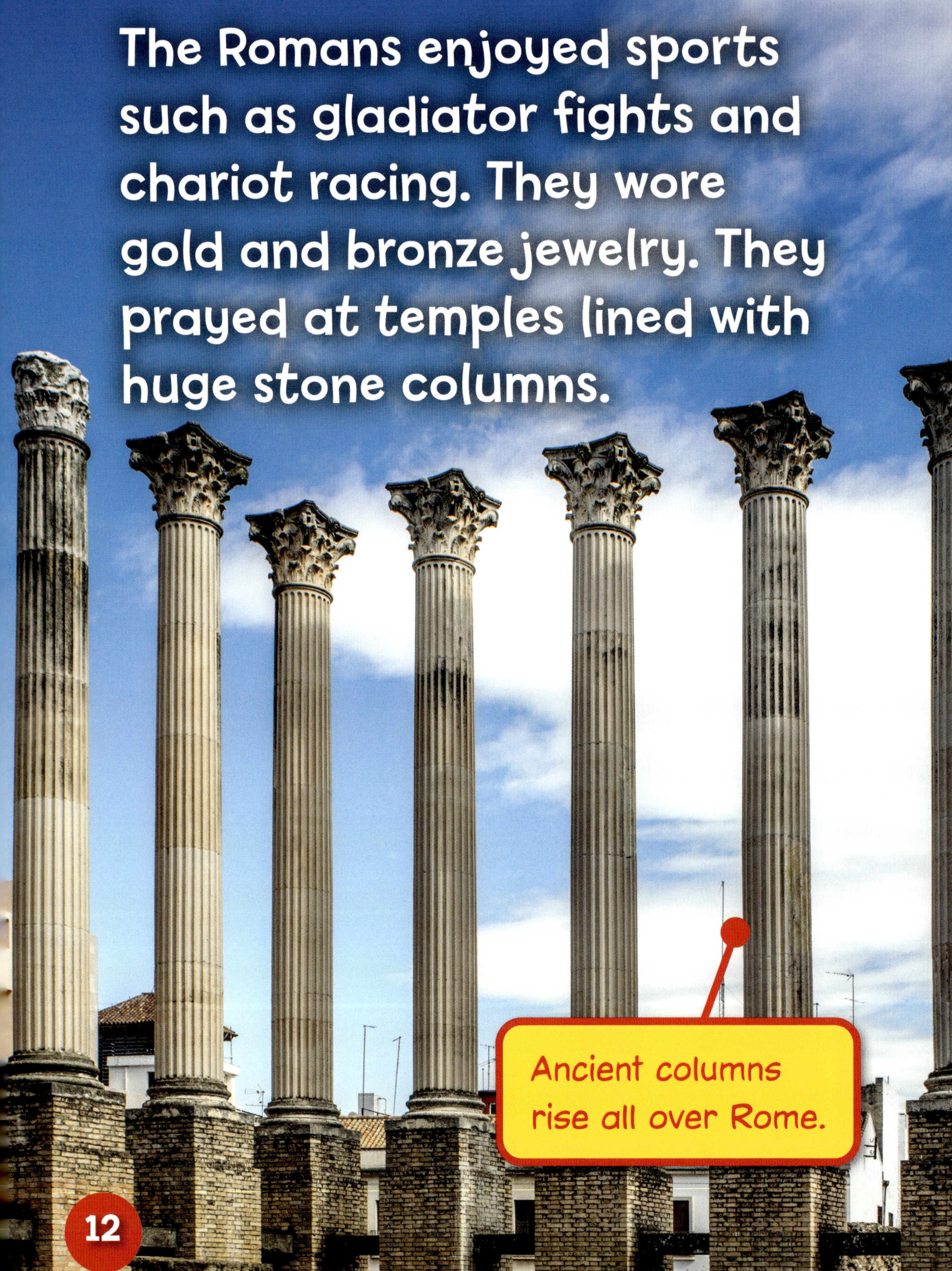

Ancient columns rise all over Rome.

Roman artists created colorful paintings of gods, people, and animals. Sculptors carved statues out of stone. Engineers built aqueducts to carry water into the city.

At first, Romans believed in many gods. But as time went on, more people began believing in one Christian God. Christianity became Rome's official religion about seventeen hundred years ago.

Jupiter was the Roman king of the gods before Christianity.

Rome's main language was Latin. Many modern languages are based on it. These include Italian, French, and Spanish.

Roman coins had Latin writing on them.

Fall of Rome

Rome was powerful for hundreds of years. But not everyone liked being part of the empire. Some of its people fought against the rulers.

The empire split in two about sixteen hundred years ago. Rome ruled the western half, and Constantinople ruled the east. Constantinople was a city in what we now call Turkey.

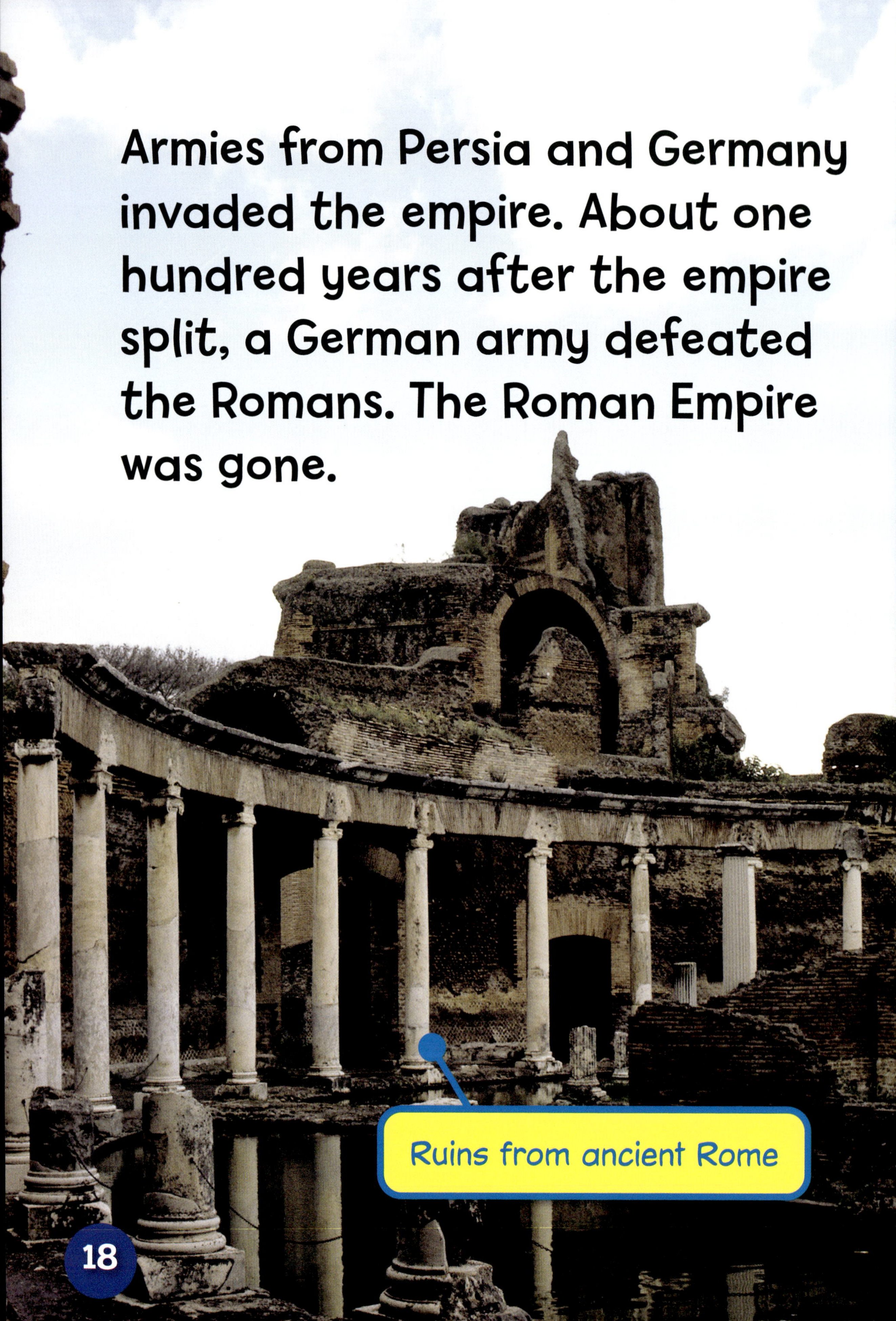

Armies from Persia and Germany invaded the empire. About one hundred years after the empire split, a German army defeated the Romans. The Roman Empire was gone.

Ruins from ancient Rome

The Roman Empire fell. But the city of Rome and its people remained. **Rome is home to more than two million people.**

A Look at Gladiators

Trained fighters called gladiators battled in arenas such as the Colosseum. Thousands of Romans gathered to watch. Gladiators fought animals, criminals, and one another. Sometimes only one gladiator survived. The winner received palm branches and money. The best gladiators became famous around the empire.

Ancient Rome Facts

- The months July and August are named after two Roman emperors: Julius and Augustus Caesar.
- The Colosseum could seat sixty thousand people.
- Rich Romans sometimes ate flamingo tongues.

Glossary

ancient: very old

aqueduct: a series of pipes, channels, and tunnels built to carry water long distances

bronze: a type of metal made of copper and tin

chariot: a vehicle pulled by horses

civilization: a large group of people who share a culture and government

column: a pillar that helps hold up a building

empire: a large area where people are ruled by one person

gladiator: a type of professional fighter

senator: someone who is elected to make laws

Learn More

BBC: What Was Life like in Ancient Rome?
https://www.bbc.co.uk/bitesize/articles/z2sm6sg

Havemeyer, Janie. *A Day in Ancient Rome*. Jump!, 2025.

History for Kids: Roman Empire Facts for Kids
https://historyforkids.org/roman-empire/

Leaf, Christina. *Rome*. Bellwether Media, 2024.

National Geographic Kids: Ancient Rome
https://kids.nationalgeographic.com/history/article/ancient-rome

Wagner, Zelda. *Explore Ancient Greece*. Lerner Publications, 2026.

Index

Photo Acknowledgments

Image credits: Julian Elliott Photography/Getty Images, p. 4; Gary Yeowell/Getty Images, p. 5; Stefano Bianchetti/Corbis via Getty Images, p. 6; Gary L. Todd, Ph.D., Professor of History, Sias International University, Xinzheng, China, p. 7; Laura Westlund/Independent Picture Service, p. 8; Cesare Maccari via Palazzo Madama (Public Domain), p. 9; DeAgostini/Getty Images, p. 10; The Walters Art Museum, p. 11; Felipe Rodriguez/VW Pics/Universal Images Group via Getty Images, p. 12; Rogers Fund, 1903, Metropolitan Museum of Art, p. 13; The Art Collector/Print Collector/Getty Images, p. 14; Gift of Martin A. Ryerson, The Art Institute of Chicago, p. 15; Hulton Archive/Getty Images, p. 16; Ayhan Altun/Getty Images, p. 17; A.A.M. Van der Heyden/Independent Picture Service, p. 18; Nico De Pasquale Photography/Getty Images, p. 19; Ken Welsh/Design Pics/Universal Images Group via Getty Images, p. 20.

Cover: lupengyu/Getty Images.